W9-COA-071

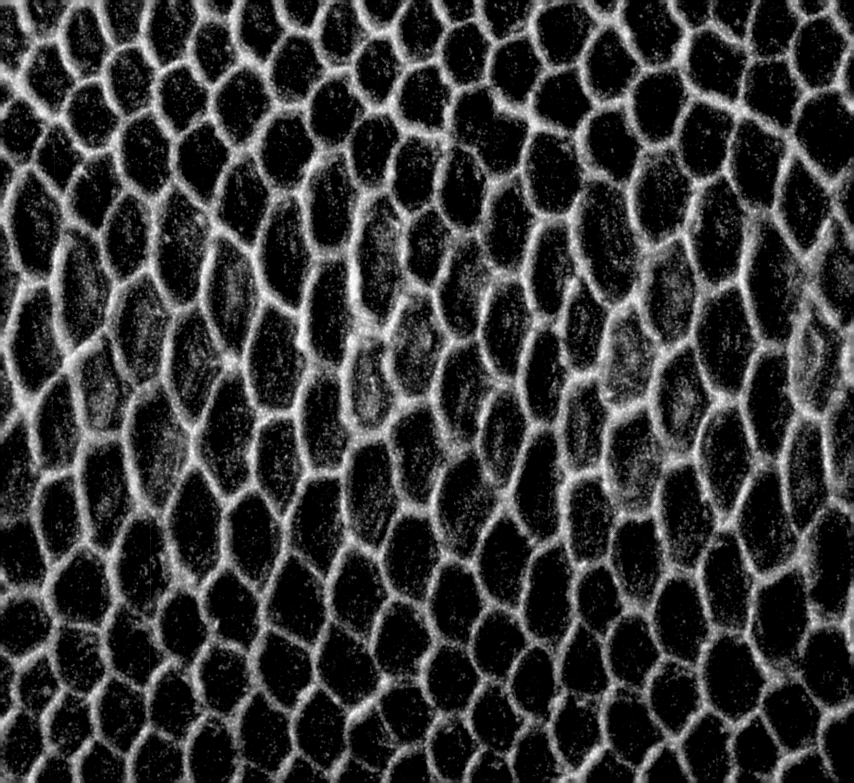

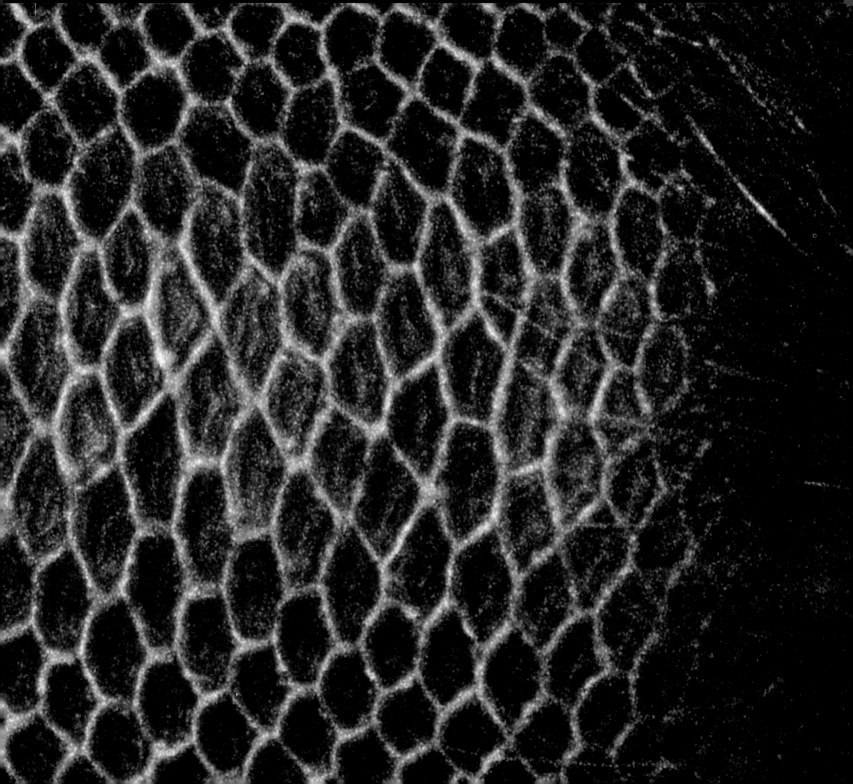

Copyright © 1987 by Michael Neugebauer Verlag AG, Gossau Zürich, Switzerland
First published in Switzerland under the title DAS BIBER-KINDER-BUCH

All rights reserved. No part of this book may be reproduced or utilized in any form
or by any means, electronic or mechanical, including photocopying, recording, or
any information storage and retrieval system, without permission in writing
from the publisher.

First published in the United States by Picture Book Studio Ltd.
Reissued in paperback in 1999 by North-South Books,
an imprint of Nord-Süd Verlag AG, Gossau Zürich, Switzerland.

Library of Congress Cataloging-in-Publication Data
Kalas, Sybille.
The beaver family book.
Translation of: Das Biber-Kinder-Buch.
Summary: Text and photographs portray the activities of three baby beavers
while being cared for by the authors/photographers for more than two years.
1. Beaver—Juvenile literature. 2. Beavers. I. Kalas, Kalas. II. Title
2. QL737.R632K3513 1987 599.32'32 87-13914

A CIP catalogue record for this book is available from The British Library.

ISBN 0-7358-1211-X
10 9 8 7 6 5 4 3 2 1
Printed in Italy

Ask your bookseller for these other North-South Animal Family Books:
THE CHIMPANZEE FAMILY BOOK by Jane Goodall
THE CROCODILE FAMILY BOOK by Mark Deeble and Victoria Stone
THE DESERT FOX FAMILY BOOK by Hans Gerold Laukel
THE ELEPHANT FAMILY BOOK by Oria Douglas-Hamilton
THE GRIZZLY BEAR FAMILY BOOK by Michio Hoshino
THE LEOPARD FAMILY BOOK by Jonathan Scott
THE LION FAMILY BOOK by Angelika Hofer and Gunter Ziesler
THE PENGUIN FAMILY BOOK by Lauritz Somme and Sybille Kalas
THE POLAR BEAR FAMILY BOOK by Sybille Kalas and Thor Larsen
THE WHALE FAMILY BOOK by Cynthia D'Vincent
THE WILD HORSE FAMILY BOOK by Sybille Kalas

For more information about our books, and the authors and artists who create them,
visit our web site: http://www.northsouth.com

Sybille and
Klaus Kalas

The Beaver
Family
Book

Translated by Patricia Crampton

A MICHAEL NEUGEBAUER BOOK
NORTH-SOUTH BOOKS / NEW YORK / LONDON

Day is dawning in beaver land.
From still, clear lakes and lonely forests,
the morning mists are rising.
Soon they will dissolve under a
brilliant blue sky.

This is Klaus. Today he is setting off on his first walk into beaver land. Shall we go with him?

You will meet the beavers, the big rodents that the Indians call "Little Brother of Man." They were building lodges and dams long before human beings learned to do so.

Come on, let's take this narrow path. It was opened by beavers . . .

It ends at a little hidden forest lake, home of a beaver family.

Once only a small stream ran here. Then beavers moved in and began to pile up twigs, stones and mud at a shallow place where the water rippled over the pebbles. Soon a small pond appeared above the dam, widening steadily into a lake as the beavers raised the height of the barrier. Now the firmly wedged twigs and branches have grown into a strong building, and the lake gives the beavers protection against enemies. It also provides a storehouse for their winter supplies of willow, birch and poplar twigs, to which they can swim safely from the entrance of their lodge under the winter covering of ice. Have you spotted the beavers' lodge yet?

The lodge has been built back there at the edge of the forest, close to the lake shore, because the entrance must always be under water, where it cannot be reached by any enemy of the beavers, except otters. Foxes, wolves or bears would get nowhere if they tried to dig into a beaver lodge from the top, because the roof is a confused tangle of strong branches and twigs. Right inside, however, this structure encloses a comfortable, dry, warm and softly-lined sleeping chamber for the whole beaver family. A passage leads to the feeding chamber, the floor of which always lies just above the water level, because beavers like to eat by the water. From here the beavers dive into an underwater passage which ends in the lake outside. If we wait patiently on the lake shore, without moving, a beaver may appear. He will swim across the lake in a glittering trail of little waves, and if we are very lucky indeed he may come ashore not far away.

Now take a look at the beaver: the broad, flat rudder of a tail, covered with scales; the big hind feet with webs between the toes; the skilful little hands; the strong, orange gnawing teeth; and the thick, brown beaver pelt. What happens when the beavers build their lodge and work on their dam? How do they fell trees and transport the wood to the building site?

What does a beaver do, deep inside the lodge? To know the answers, one would have to become a beaver oneself, and that is exactly what Klaus intends to do. He has decided to become a "mother" to three beaver children.

But where can young beavers be found? In a place where there are still many of them: northern Sweden. Here beavers are protected by the forest keepers and naturalists who study and observe them. We have been given special permission to transfer three baby beavers from Sweden to Austria, in the hopes of reintroducing beavers to a place where they once lived.

When we find a beaver lodge and start digging, the beaver parents will dive into the pond very quietly, unnoticed by us, to find a safe place to hide until we are gone. They will leave their babies behind in the lodge, because they know instinctively that no animal can dig through to the inside. But with our tools, we will be able to gently open the sleeping chamber and lift out the beaver babies.

When the parents return they will find an empty sleeping chamber. We do not really know if the parents will look for their young, but we do know that when animals find empty nests – because of the accidents, illness, and death that often occur in the wild – they just move ahead with the next part of their lives. These beavers will soon set about getting their lodge back in order. But of course, the young beavers we will find will not come to any harm. Though the beaver parents cannot know it, their babies will be loved and cared for and studied. Taking young beavers from their homes and bringing them to a place where we can study them is the only way to make sure that beavers continue to live in a place where they have started to vanish.

In June, the middle of springtime in northern Sweden, we will set off to look for Klaus's future beaver children. Would you like to come along?

Now at long last we have found what we were looking for! Climb very quietly and carefully onto the beaver lodge, put your ear to it and listen, as Klaus is listening now. Can you hear the beaver babies in their sleeping-chamber? Can you hear their high-pitched squeaks and grunts? It is easy to picture them now, butting hungrily at their mother's teats.

Now we can set about opening up the lodge. We shall have to be very careful not to frighten the little beavers. We have already found the entrance to the sleeping chamber. Klaus pushes his head and arms through the narrow opening…

Darkness and warmth envelop him along with the smell of beaver – a unique, pleasantly tangy scent, that reminds you of autumn glades, the river and the lake…

Klaus's searching hands feel the floor of the sleeping chamber, lined with dry wood chips, still warm from the beavers which have slept there. And then, in a corner, his fingers brush over three little balls of fur, cuddled close together – his beaver babies!

Here they are, and all three are going to have names. We call them "Laurie," after a Swedish friend; "Hector," the rather hectic, nervous, sensitive one; and "Midge," the only female of the three.

They will grow up here at Beaverbrook in Austria, far from where they were born. They will teach us a great deal about the family life of beavers, their "language" and their nightly work of felling trees and building a dam and a lodge. Will they turn their new home into beaver land? That would be nice!

We have prepared a beaver home for them in Klaus's hut, with a sleeping and a feeding chamber, where they can be observed through a window. An underwater passage leads out to the pool, edged with many of the trees and plants that beavers like to eat.

But for the time being none of this means as much to the three babies as Klaus: Klaus, with his milk bottle, and Klaus who strokes, scratches and fondles them; Klaus, who talks to them, and Klaus who cuddles up with them in their sleeping chamber; Klaus, who is their new mother.

There are lots of things to get used to – things that are different from the Swedish beaver lodge. In particular, there is the new milk, which is really meant for puppies, and the unfamiliar bottle, made for human babies. Where could Klaus find a rubber nipple that would feel like the long, thin teat of a beaver? Klaus needs time and patience to convince his babies that milk can be drunk from a baby's bottle. Now they crowd around it with the same demanding, hungry voices we heard from them before, in the beaver lodge in Sweden.

As soon as they wake up in their sleeping chamber, their cheerful faces appear at the observation window. Out they climb, and waddle across the hut like little goblins on their broad, webbed feet.

When they are feeling particularly boisterous they perform their "beaver dance," waving their heads and bounding to and fro. Midge has taken over Klaus's bed. She looks as if she were laughing!

And there, on the bed that smells so sweetly of their beaver "mother," they fall asleep. Often just one little beaver nose pokes out of Klaus's sleeping bag.

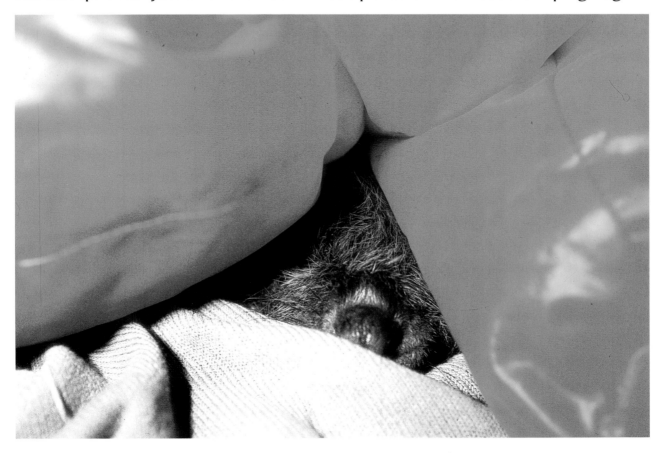

They really like to climb into the bag early in the morning, when Klaus has just gone to bed after a long night of observation. Can you imagine what it feels like to have a wet beaver creeping under your bedclothes and snuggling down with you?

As soon as they wake up, they are hungry again. They bounce along behind Klaus in a beaver gallop and reach up, balancing on their hind feet and tails, to demand food.

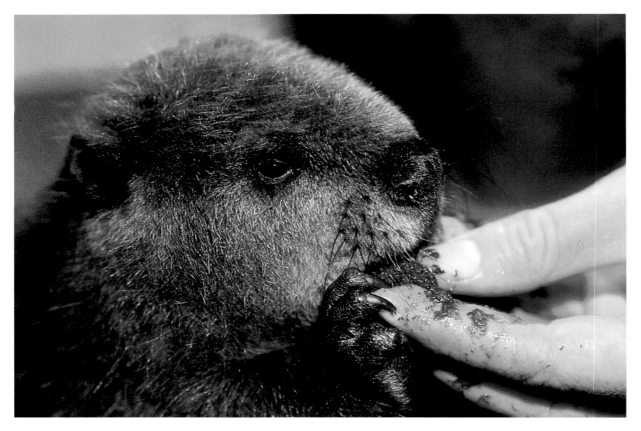

They are particularly fond of a kind of salad made of plants that beavers like, such as sow-thistle, stinging nettles, and meadow-sweet, which they eat from Klaus's hand, smacking their lips loudly with pleasure.

The little balls of fur have already turned into proper young beavers, but they still like their milk bottle. Hector has stolen a nipple and run off with it. Now he lies sucking at it, though he too can eat willow leaves like his brother Laurie.

Look how well he uses his little paws to hold the twigs, turning the larger ones around deftly and gnawing off the bark. Then, sappy shoots are pushed lengthwise between his rodent's gnawing teeth and nibbled up at astonishing speed. Beavers can gnaw quite easily, even under water, because they can shut their mouths behind the gnawing teeth, and their nostrils and ears, too!

Just before they fall asleep, or when they wake up, feeling quite secure in their snug sleeping chamber, beavers love to clean and nibble each other's fur. The sounds they make then are soft and friendly and quite high-pitched.

This is when Klaus realizes that he is not a real beaver, after all.
What beavers feel as gentle nibbling is distinctly painful to Klaus's beard, and a beaver's coat-cleaning methods leave big holes in a man's sweater!

They learned some time ago to dive out to the pool through the exit from the artificial beaver lodge. When Klaus calls to them from the bank they come swimming up and greet him with friendly, high-pitched sounds. Then, wet as they are, they clamber up to see if he has one or two apples or carrots for them. Of course he has, and they pester him with excited beaver grunts, only to make off again not long afterwards to one of the little bays around the pond…

…and over there on the bank, on islands and peninsulas and along the stream, they go about their beaver work. Just as if they had done it a thousand times before, they fell willows, birches and poplars with their razor-sharp rodent teeth.

Soon we can see the evidence of their hard work everywhere.

With one bite of their strong rodent teeth they cut off twigs from the felled trees and drag them to the lakeside. There you can see all three of them sitting close together, eating leaves and bark.

Our beavers are now two years old. You will be surprised to see how much they have built. They were obviously not entirely happy with our artificial beaver lodge, because they immediately built two new real beaver lodges of their own in front of Klaus's hut. The lodges were built up gradually through many nights of hard work.

Every night, under the searchlights, you can see Laurie, Midge and Hector working. They waddle tirelessly on their big hind feet from pond to lodge, carrying big loads of mud, stones and branches clamped between paws and chin.

Once there, they unload their burden, wedge the branches in and spread the mud with thrusting movements of their paws. As soon as they have used all the building materials they are off to the pond again to hoist the next load from the bottom to the building site.

They thought so little of the dam we had made at the end of the pond that they set about turning it into a real beaver dam. At the points where water was flowing out they added strong branches brought from a long distance. The dam that stands there now is already higher, thicker and stronger than our old one and can actually be used as a bridge.

As the dam grew, the pool widened. It has become a large, still beaver lake, flooding part of the surrounding woodland. Through the work of our beaver children a new beaver land has been created, which may become the home of a large beaver family.

If they were still living with their parents in Sweden, it would now be time for the young beavers to leave the lodge and seek mates and make lodges of their own at a lake or a river. When a beaver looks for a mate, he always tries to find one other than his own brother or sister, if he can. Here at Beaverbrook there are no other beavers, but we are still hoping for a beaver family. And it looks as if our hopes are going to be fulfilled.

Since last winter the two male beavers have not been able to bear one another's company. As soon as they meet they hiss furiously at each other and often start such a fight that the water foams and the spray flies. Hector, the weaker of the two, soon retreats to an isolated bay.

Midge and Laurie have become a pair, and they can always be seen together now. Since there are no parents already living in the lodge, it has become their home. Snuggled close together, they sleep in the lodge, and can often be seen nibbling and cleaning each other's fur, or eating their meals peacefully side-by-side on the bank.

And what do you think happened today?
Put your ear close to the beaver lodge and you will hear a familiar voice: that's right! A beaver baby, talking to its mother. Midge has had her first baby!

The little beaver is still a ball of fur with a shiny black tail not much bigger than a man's thumb. He still lives in the shelter of the lodge, under the tender care of his mother and father. But soon he will be swimming out into the twilight of the beaver land . . .
We wish him luck!

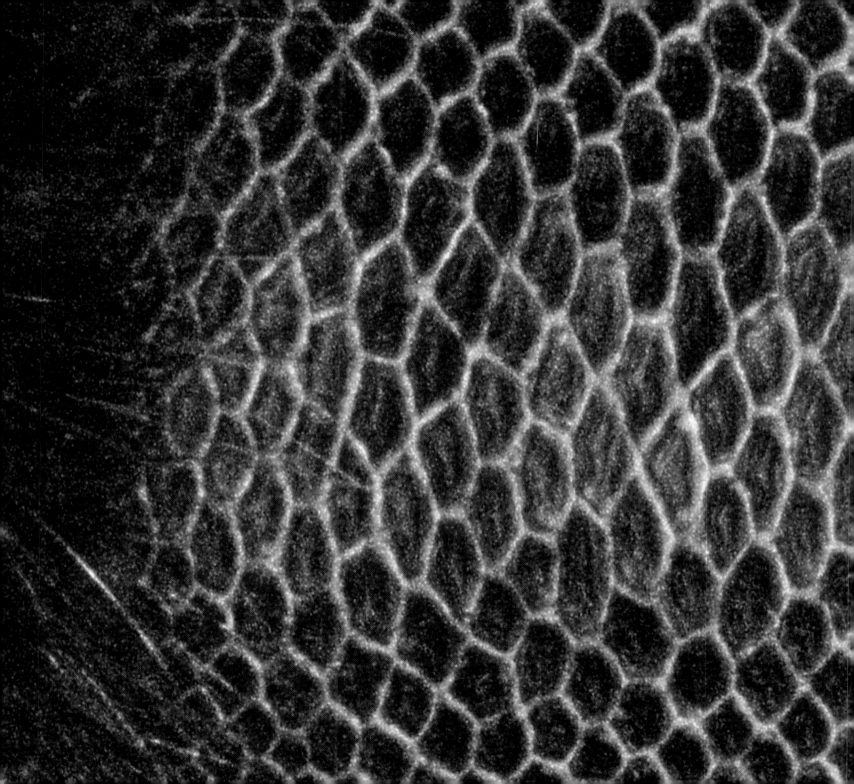

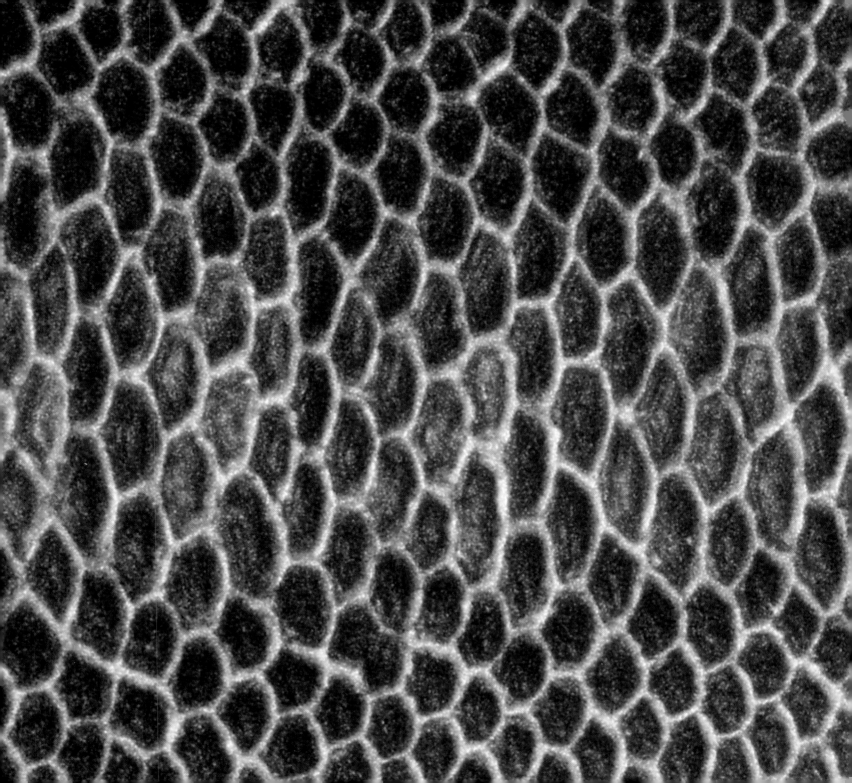